W9-BYO-516

TABLE OF CONTENTS

Stocks

How to Reduce Risk and Get Your Money's Worth

MOODY PRESS
CHICAGO

© 1994 by
AUSTIN PRYOR

All rights reserved. No part of this book may be reproduced in any form without permission in writing from the publisher, except in the case of brief quotations embodied in critical articles or reviews.

All Scripture quotations, unless indicated, are taken from the *Holy Bible: New International Version*. Copyright © 1973, 1978, 1984, International Bible Society. Used by permission of Zondervan Publishing House. All rights reserved.

ISBN 0-8024-3990-X

Library of Congress Cataloging in Publication Data

1 3 5 7 9 10 8 6 4 2

Printed in the United States of America

FOREWORD

I have known Austin Pryor for almost twenty years now, and I regard him as a good friend. As I have observed him over the years, I have found his counsel to be both biblical and practical. I know of no other individual with whom I would consult with more confidence on the subject of mutual fund investing than Austin.

I believe the true character of an investment adviser is not only the degree of success he has achieved, but the integrity that is maintained in the process. Austin has achieved success in the business world, but, more important, he has done so with truth and honesty.

Obviously you, the reader, must evaluate his advice yourself. No one individual has the right advice for everyone, and anyone can, and will, be wrong in the changing economy we live in. But if you will spend the time to read carefully the counsel Austin provides, you will find it both time and money well spent.

I encouraged my good friends at Moody Press to contact Austin about publishing his writing because I felt he had information that would benefit God's people. We are in no way competitors. Austin and I are collaborators in God's plan to help His people become better stewards of His resources.

Larry Burkett

The biblical principles reflected in this booklet are the foundation for the advice given in *Sound Mind Investing*, my book published by Moody Press. The material in this booklet has, for the most part, been excerpted from that book. As Christians, we acknowledge God as the owner of all. We serve as His stewards with management privileges and responsibilities. The practical application of biblical principles leads us to encourage a debt-free lifestyle and conservative approach to investing such as that shown in what we call the Four Levels of Investing:

Level One: Getting Debt-Free
"The rich rules over the poor, and the borrower becomes the lender's slave."
Proverbs 22:7

Paying off debts which are carrying 12%-18% per year interest charges is the best "investment" move you can make. So, get to work on paying off those credit cards, car loans, student loans, and other short-term debts. Accelerating the payments on your house mortgage, if any, should also be your goal—albeit a longer-term one. It should be your first priority to see the day when you're meeting all current living expenses, supporting the Lord's causes, and completely free of consumer debt.

Level Two: Saving for Future Needs
"There is precious treasure and oil in the dwelling of the wise, but a foolish man swallows it up." *Proverbs 21:20*

Even if you've not completely reached your Level One goal, it's still a good idea to set aside some money for emergencies or large purchases. A prudent rule of thumb is that your contingency fund should be equal to three to six months living expenses. We suggest $10,000 as an amount suitable for most family situations.

Level Three: Investing in Stocks
*"Well done, good and faithful servant. You were faithful with a few things,
I will put you in charge of many things." Matthew 25:21*

Only money you have saved over and above the funds set aside in
Level 2 should be considered for investing in the stock market. In
Levels One and Two, any monthly surplus was used in a manner
that *guaranteed* you would advance financially—there are no guar-
antees in the stock market. You should initiate a program of stock
mutual fund investing geared to your personal risk temperament
and the amount of dollars you have available to invest.

Level Four: Diversifying for Safety
*"Divide your portion to seven, or even to eight, for you do not know what
misfortune may occur on the earth." Ecclesiastes 11:2*

Once you accumulate $25,000 in your investment account, it's time
for further diversification. By adding investments to your holdings
that "march to different drummers," you can create a more efficient,
less volatile portfolio. The single most important diversification
decision is deciding how much to invest in stocks versus bonds.
That's why determining your personal investing temperament, and
following the guidelines given, can be so helpful.

Free Upon Request

Articles that guide you through the Four Levels—help on getting
debt-free, saving strategies, and updates on specific no-load mutual
fund recommendations that are geared to your personal risk tolerance—appear in my monthly newsletter, also called *Sound Mind
Investing*. In it, I offer a conservative investing strategy based on the
careful use of no-load mutual funds. For a free sample copy, simply
return the postage-paid card included at the back of this booklet.

Understanding the Risk and Rewards of Investing by Owning

1

I. **Inflation is the single greatest threat to your financial well-being.**

   A. Inflation increased at a rate of 6.2% per year during the past decade, as measured by the consumer price index.

   B. The primary cause of inflation is deficit spending by the federal government.

   C. The elimination of deficit spending and the national debt are not likely, so inflation will continue to eat into your purchasing power.

II. **Overcoming inflation requires being an owner rather than a lender.**

   A. Lenders are more vulnerable to inflation because they are locked into the economic conditions that prevail at the time they make their loans. By using your investment capital to take ownership of an asset that has practical utility and inherent value, you are no longer linked to the fate of paper currency.

B. We will take a look at the historical performance of six different assets you can own: common stocks, gold, silver, commercial real estate, single-family homes, farmland, and oil.

"Dad, today I bought all these baseball cards at the flea market for $15, and my catalog says they're worth $25! I've already made $10!"

Have you ever tried explaining to your children that a thing is worth only what someone is willing to pay for it? And that unless they intend to become dealers in baseball cards, it's highly unlikely they will even be able to get their $15 back, let alone gain $10 in profits? My boys simply brushed off such explanations as being naive and hopelessly out of touch with the financial realities governing baseball cards (or stamps, or comic books, or whatever they were collecting at the time), which apparently are exempt from the normal rules governing commerce. The fact that I had a college degree in economics and was a full-fledged investment adviser carried no weight whatsoever. They regarded me with a kind of bemused tolerance ("Poor dad, he means well.").

Children aren't the only ones who sometimes have a difficult time with the concept of value. Grown-ups do, too, and one reason is that the value of money keeps changing on us. If you tell today's kids that "a penny saved is a penny earned," their response may well be, "So what?" If Ben Franklin were with us today to bring his dictum up-to-date, he'd have to say, "16¢ saved is 16¢ earned," just to take into account the inflation we've had this century alone.

Inflation is not well understood by the general public. We think of it as meaning things cost more. Actually, it's because...

...our dollar is worth less. As the government "inflates" the number of dollars being passed around by printing billions and billions more than is justified by America's real economic growth, the value of each individual dollar is diluted. This is what decades of federal government deficit spending have accomplished. So the problem is more accurately described as one of "shrinkage."

The U.S. Department of Labor helps us keep track of how bad this shrinkage is by collecting data on about 100,000 prices—everything from the cost of apples to gasoline to housing—and weights them to reflect a typical family's spending patterns.

It updates its findings each month and releases them in what is known as the consumer price index (CPI). Unfortunately, the accuracy of the CPI has become suspect. The government has a vested interest in keeping the "official" inflation rate as low as possible. That's because increases in the CPI cause changes in payments under all sorts of agreements ranging from labor contracts to Social Security and other pension benefits. Also, because higher inflation leads to higher interest rates, the cost of interest on the national debt can rise dramatically, making the federal budget deficit problem even worse.

INFLATION IN THE U.S.
OVER THE PAST 50 YEARS

This table is based on the 1982-84 series of consumer prices. That means the index uses the number "100" to represent the average cost of living during those years. One way of expressing the December 1993 reading of 145.8 is to say, "In late 1993, it cost $145.80 to purchase what $100.00 would buy in mid-1983." Or, "In 1943, you could pay $17.40 to get what cost $145.80 in late 1993."

Year	Index	Year	Index	Year	Index
1943	17.4	1960	29.8	1977	62.1
1944	17.8	1961	30.0	1978	67.7
1945	18.2	1962	30.4	1979	76.7
1946	21.5	1963	30.9	1980	86.3
1947	23.4	1964	31.2	1981	94.0
1948	24.1	1965	31.8	1982	97.6
1949	23.6	1966	32.9	1983	101.3
1950	25.0	1967	33.9	1984	105.3
1951	26.5	1968	35.5	1985	109.3
1952	26.7	1969	37.7	1986	110.5
1953	26.9	1970	39.8	1987	115.4
1954	26.7	1971	41.1	1988	120.5
1955	26.8	1972	42.5	1989	126.1
1956	27.6	1973	46.2	1990	133.8
1957	28.4	1974	51.9	1991	137.9
1958	28.9	1975	55.5	1992	141.9
1959	29.4	1976	58.2	1993	145.8

These pressures may be the reason government officials occasionally change the way the CPI is computed. Of course...

...they do this under the guise of making it more accurate or "representative." However, the changes always have the effect of lowering, rather than raising, the numbers. For example, in the 1980s they stopped including the cost of new automobiles in the CPI. The justification was that since new models always have improvements, you can't really compare a new car to last year's model. Besides, you don't buy a new car every year. Likewise, when housing payments began to rise, they took them out. Not everyone has a mortgage, they said.

This kind of tampering leads to a second misunderstanding about inflation: Your "personal" inflation experience might be much higher than the "official" inflation rate.

The official rate has been troublesome enough. At the end of 1971, the consumer price index was 41.1. Twenty years later, it stood at 137.9. That translates to an average official inflation rate of 6.2% per year. Or, stated in terms that are more understandable (and more shocking), a 1971 dollar has officially shrunk to just 30 cents! Some economists maintain that the true rate of inflation has actually been much worse. One consulting firm calculated it to be 12.2%, a national accounting firm came up with 15.0%, and the editor of the

nation's largest financial newsletter for re-
tirees places the inflation rate at 13.9%.

An analysis of U.S. inflation rates this century shows a shift in severity starting two
decades ago. From 1900 through 1971, the
average annual rate of inflation was 2.24%.
Then in 1971, the U.S. abandoned its last ves-
tiges of commitment to the gold standard

THE AMAZING GROWTH
OF AMERICA'S ANNUAL
FEDERAL BUDGET
DEFICITS

"We should consider ourselves unauthorized to
saddle posterity with our debts, and morally
bound to pay them ourselves."

Thomas Jefferson

Estimated at $340
billion for 1993.
Is this insane, or what?

1946
1948
1950
1952
1954
1956
1958
1960
1962
1964
1966
1968
1970
1972 — Final
       abandonment
1974   of the gold
       standard
1976
1978
1980
1982
1984
1986
1988
1990
1992

$0 $100 $200 $300
BILLIONS PER YEAR ADDED TO THE NATIONAL DEBT

(see glossary). Without the discipline imposed by the gold standard, there was nothing left to prevent the federal government from printing as much money as it can dream up ways to spend (which is more or less what they've been doing ever since). The graph on page 12 shows the amount of the annual federal budget deficits of the past forty years. You'll see that the budget came close to being in balance, give or take a few billion here and there, up until the early 1970s. Do you think it's a coincidence that our federal budget deficit problems began in earnest shortly after we left the gold standard? Since that time, the annual average rate of inflation has been 6.24%. It would have been even greater but for other anti-inflationary developments such as the recession of 1990-1991 and the break-up of the Organization of Petroleum Exporting Countries (OPEC).

In light of the defeat by Congress of the proposed balanced budget amendment in 1992 (despite very high public support for such a measure), there is no reason to expect Washington to muster the needed political willpower to effectively deal with the budget deficits in the near future.

So, what can you do to protect your purchasing power and keep ahead of inflation? One thing you don't want to do...

...is get locked into long-term fixed income investments. If you're not going to be a lender, your other alternative is to be an owner. By being an owner, you exchange something of theoretical value (paper currency) for something of inherent value like land, buildings, precious metals, or petroleum. Or you can become part owner of a business that owns these things. By doing this, your investment becomes linked with changing economic conditions, whereas lenders are locked into the conditions that prevailed on the day they made the loan, plus their investments are always measured in terms of paper dollars.

When you acquire ownership of something that has a practical usefulness, that asset becomes your new "money." Unlike paper dollars, it has intrinsic value...

...that stems from the practical ways it can be used. Land can grow crops, a house can provide shelter, metals have industrial uses, and oil is needed worldwide on a massive scale. You have broken the chain that linked you to the fate of the dollar. When you convert the asset back into dollars, it will be valued in terms of what the dollar is worth *at that time*. If you have invested wisely, the amount of dollars you get back when you sell your ownership rights will have at least as much, and hopefully more, purchasing power as the dollars you spent to acquire the asset in the first place.

On the following pages, you will find *inflation-adjusted* performance histories of various kinds of equity-type investments. *The returns shown are called "real" returns because they are the gains left after inflation has been taken into account.* The returns suggest the advisability of "investing by owning." ◆

Blue Chip Stocks

(As noted in The 1992 Chase Investment Performance Digest)

The 30 stocks within the Dow Jones average are the bluest of the blue chips. Today's examples are: American Telephone, General Motors, IBM, and General Electric. All of these companies pay a regular dividend and rarely run into financial problems. However, occasionally Dow Jones Industrial companies have had financial difficulties that have affected the performance of the overall Average. Thus there are times when even this ultimate blue chip average is impacted by a member's significantly less than blue chip corporate performance. The Standard & Poor's (S&P) 500 Stock Index, a broader measure of large companies, is less affected by the movements of just a few stocks. Over time, however, the Dow and S&P have generally performed similarly.

THE DOW JONES INDUSTRIAL AVERAGE
(ANNUALIZED RETURNS MINUS INFLATION FOR VARIOUS FIVE YEAR HOLDING PERIODS)

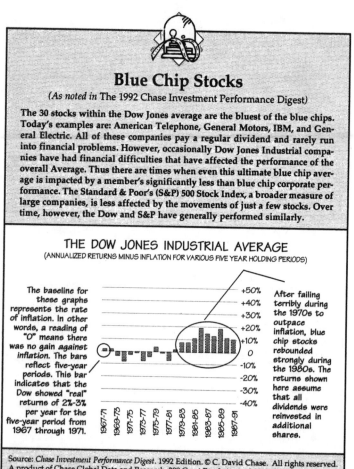

The baseline for these graphs represents the rate of inflation. In other words, a reading of "0" means there was no gain against inflation. The bars reflect five-year periods. This bar indicates that the Dow showed "real" returns of 2%-3% per year for the five-year period from 1967 through 1971.

After failing terribly during the 1970s to outpace inflation, blue chip stocks rebounded strongly during the 1980s. The returns shown here assume that all dividends were reinvested in additional shares.

+50%
+40%
+30%
+20%
+10%
0
-10%
-20%
-30%
-40%

1967-71
1969-73
1971-75
1973-77
1975-79
1977-81
1979-83
1981-85
1983-87
1985-89
1987-91

Source: *Chase Investment Performance Digest.* 1992 Edition. © C. David Chase. All rights reserved. A product of Chase Global Data and Research, 289 Great Road, Acton, MA 01720. (508) 263-0404. Although gathered from reliable sources, data accuracy and completeness cannot be guaranteed.

Smaller Growth Stocks

(As noted in The 1992 Chase Investment Performance Digest)

John and Jane Doe do not typically hold only the blue chip securities (Dow Industrials), nor do they exclusively purchase shares in the nation's 500 largest companies (S&P 500). There are more than 7,000 others to choose from, among which might be the next IBM or GE. In reality, investors hold a mix of stocks from the major exchanges as well as the over-the-counter market. One of the better indicators for tracking the equity portfolios held by the proverbial "average" investor is the Value Line Composite Index, a mix of about 1,700 common stocks. At the start of 1992, the Value Line Composite Index was represented by the following marketplaces: 70% New York Stock Exchange, 22% Over-the-Counter, 5% American Stock Exchange, and 3% on Canadian Exchanges.

THE VALUE LINE COMPOSITE INDEX
ANNUALIZED RETURNS LESS INFLATION FOR VARIOUS FIVE YEAR PERIODS

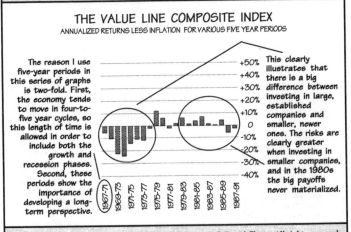

The reason I use five-year periods in this series of graphs is two-fold. First, the economy tends to move in four-to-five year cycles, so this length of time is allowed in order to include both the growth and recession phases. Second, these periods show the importance of developing a long-term perspective.

This clearly illustrates that there is a big difference between investing in large, established companies and smaller, newer ones. The risks are clearly greater when investing in smaller companies, and in the 1980s the big payoffs never materialized.

Source: *Chase Investment Performance Digest.* 1992 Edition. © C. David Chase. All rights reserved. A product of Chase Global Data and Research, 289 Great Road, Acton, MA 01720. (508) 263-0404. Although gathered from reliable sources, data accuracy and completeness cannot be guaranteed.

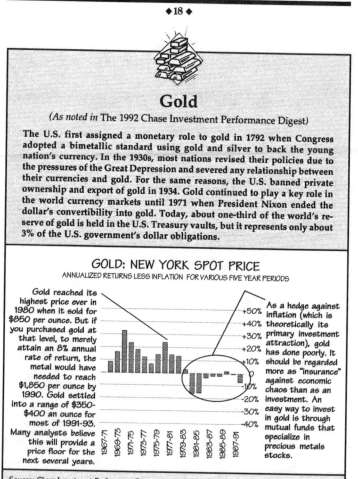

Gold

(As noted in The 1992 Chase Investment Performance Digest)

The U.S. first assigned a monetary role to gold in 1792 when Congress adopted a bimetallic standard using gold and silver to back the young nation's currency. In the 1930s, most nations revised their policies due to the pressures of the Great Depression and severed any relationship between their currencies and gold. For the same reasons, the U.S. banned private ownership and export of gold in 1934. Gold continued to play a key role in the world currency markets until 1971 when President Nixon ended the dollar's convertibility into gold. Today, about one-third of the world's reserve of gold is held in the U.S. Treasury vaults, but it represents only about 3% of the U.S. government's dollar obligations.

GOLD: NEW YORK SPOT PRICE
ANNUALIZED RETURNS LESS INFLATION FOR VARIOUS FIVE YEAR PERIODS

Gold reached its highest price ever in 1980 when it sold for $850 per ounce. But if you purchased gold at that level, to merely attain an 8% annual rate of return, the metal would have needed to reach $1,850 per ounce by 1990. Gold settled into a range of $350-$400 an ounce for most of 1991-93. Many analysts believe this will provide a price floor for the next several years.

As a hedge against inflation (which is theoretically its primary investment attraction), gold has done poorly. It should be regarded more as "insurance" against economic chaos than as an investment. An easy way to invest in gold is through mutual funds that specialize in precious metals stocks.

Source: *Chase Investment Performance Digest.* 1992 Edition. © C. David Chase. All rights reserved. A product of Chase Global Data and Research, 289 Great Road, Acton, MA 01720. (508) 263-0404. Although gathered from reliable sources, data accuracy and completeness cannot be guaranteed.

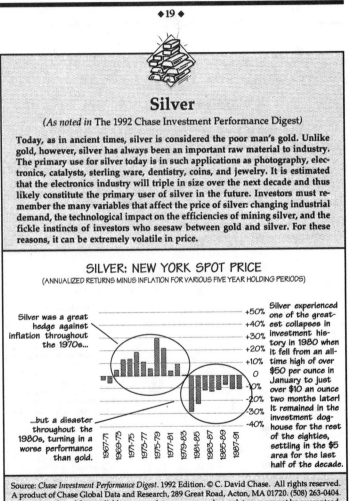

Silver

(As noted in The 1992 Chase Investment Performance Digest)

Today, as in ancient times, silver is considered the poor man's gold. Unlike gold, however, silver has always been an important raw material to industry. The primary use for silver today is in such applications as photography, electronics, catalysts, sterling ware, dentistry, coins, and jewelry. It is estimated that the electronics industry will triple in size over the next decade and thus likely constitute the primary user of silver in the future. Investors must remember the many variables that affect the price of silver: changing industrial demand, the technological impact on the efficiencies of mining silver, and the fickle instincts of investors who seesaw between gold and silver. For these reasons, it can be extremely volatile in price.

SILVER: NEW YORK SPOT PRICE

(ANNUALIZED RETURNS MINUS INFLATION FOR VARIOUS FIVE YEAR HOLDING PERIODS)

Silver was a great hedge against inflation throughout the 1970s...

...but a disaster throughout the 1980s, turning in a worse performance than gold.

+50%
+40%
+30%
+20%
+10%
0
-10%
-20%
-30%
-40%

1967-71
1969-73
1971-75
1973-77
1975-79
1977-81
1979-83
1981-85
1983-87
1985-89
1987-91

Silver experienced one of the greatest collapses in investment history in 1980 when it fell from an all-time high of over $50 per ounce in January to just over $10 an ounce two months later! It remained in the investment dog-house for the rest of the eighties, settling in the $5 area for the last half of the decade.

Source: *Chase Investment Performance Digest*. 1992 Edition. © C. David Chase. All rights reserved. A product of Chase Global Data and Research, 289 Great Road, Acton, MA 01720. (508) 263-0404. Although gathered from reliable sources, data accuracy and completeness cannot be guaranteed.

Commercial Real Estate

(As noted in The 1992 Chase Investment Performance Digest*)*

Real Estate Investment Trusts (or REITs) were authorized by Congress in the early 1960s. The goal was to provide small investors an opportunity to invest in large-scale real estate projects and to share in some of the tax benefits as well. Since then REITs have had a tumultuous and poor performance record. REITs are publicly traded securities that can be bought and sold like stocks. There are more than seventy-five REIT issues on the major exchanges and the over-the-counter markets with a total market value estimated at $10 billion. The value of shares of REITs is affected by property values, rent trends, market perceptions about real estate, and the fluctuating level of interest rates.

STANDARD & POOR'S REIT INDEX
ANNUALIZED RETURNS LESS INFLATION FOR VARIOUS FIVE YEAR PERIODS

Much like a mutual fund, the money in a REIT is invested in a diversified manner—primarily in shopping malls, office buildings, hotels, and apartment complexes. REITs offer yields that are greater than common stocks (because of their internal tax benefits).

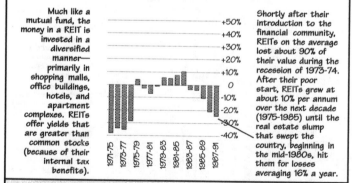

Shortly after their introduction to the financial community, REITs on the average lost about 90% of their value during the recession of 1973-74. After their poor start, REITs grew at about 10% per annum over the next decade (1975-1985) until the real estate slump that swept the country, beginning in the mid-1980s, hit them for losses averaging 16% a year.

Source: *Chase Investment Performance Digest.* 1992 Edition. © C. David Chase. All rights reserved. A product of Chase Global Data and Research, 289 Great Road, Acton, MA 01720. (508) 263-0404. Although gathered from reliable sources, data accuracy and completeness cannot be guaranteed.

Single Family Housing

(As noted in The 1992 Chase Investment Performance Digest)

Overall, the housing marketplace in the U.S. has been a consistently upward performer, especially when you consider that home ownership gives protection from wind and rain and also can provide rental income and price appreciation. But there are risks to the home's value as a result of population shifts, changes in the economy, changes in household formations, and the up and down aspects of using leverage in purchasing a home. Just as with many other investments, diversification could be the key for successful real estate investing. For that reason a close review of the regional aspects of U.S. housing is a productive exercise—the national average is not always relevant to what is happening locally.

NEW ONE-FAMILY HOUSE PRICE INDEX
ANNUALIZED RETURNS LESS INFLATION FOR VARIOUS FIVE YEAR PERIODS

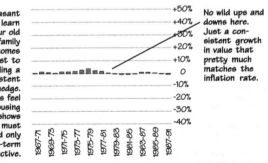

What a pleasant surprise to learn that our old friend, the family homestead, comes closest to providing a consistent inflation hedge. Most experts feel the housing market shows promise but must be viewed only from a long-term perspective.

No wild ups and downs here. Just a consistent growth in value that pretty much matches the inflation rate.

Source: *Chase Investment Performance Digest.* 1992 Edition. © C. David Chase. All rights reserved. A product of Chase Global Data and Research, 289 Great Road, Acton, MA 01720. (508) 263-0404. Although gathered from reliable sources, data accuracy and completeness cannot be guaranteed.

Farmland

(As noted in The 1992 Chase Investment Performance Digest)

From our country's inception, the U.S. has steadily developed as a strong agricultural nation capable of supplying foods, grains, and livestock at home and abroad. The number of farms peaked in 1935 and dropped by more than half over the next forty-five years. The Farmland Index, issued by the U.S. Department of Agriculture, began tracking prices in 1912, when the average acre of farmland was priced at $27. In 1991, the average value of a farmland acre in the U.S. was $682. The 1980s was a brutal decade for the small farmer—it has been estimated that more than 100,000 were forced out of business. From a long-term perspective, prices may be attractive. In that vein, one should remember Mark Twain's immortal saying about land, "They aren't making it anymore."

U.S. FARMLAND PRICE INDEX
ANNUALIZED RETURNS LESS INFLATION FOR VARIOUS FIVE YEAR PERIODS

Farmland as an investment medium has performed in a reasonable manner over the past twenty-five years, averaging growth of 6% per annum. Renting your farmland to others can yield cash rents as little as 1% or as high as 8%. The primary variable is the land's potential for appreciation, which will be the key determinant for the overall return of your investment.

By far the worst performance has occurred since 1982. Over the past ten years, prices have lost almost 2% per year. 1990's prices, after inflation, are sharply below the levels of all of the 1980s.

Chart values (vertical axis): +50%, +40%, +30%, +20%, +10%, 0, -10%, -20%, -30%, -40%

Chart periods (horizontal axis): 1967-71, 1969-73, 1971-75, 1973-77, 1975-79, 1977-81, 1979-83, 1981-85, 1983-87, 1985-89, 1987-91

Source: *Chase Investment Performance Digest*. 1992 Edition. © C. David Chase. All rights reserved.
A product of Chase Global Data and Research, 289 Great Road, Acton, MA 01720. (508) 263-0404.
Although gathered from reliable sources, data accuracy and completeness cannot be guaranteed.

Oil

(As noted in The 1992 Chase Investment Performance Digest)

The big question is: What is the future of crude oil? There is the possibility of another major find in Prudhoe Bay, Alaska, which would have a major impact on U.S. domestic oil reserves and thus reduce U.S. demand for imported oil for perhaps another decade—if the field is brought along within the next five years. There is also a new unknown in the equation—the recent discovery of superconductivity—which could someday eliminate the need for most internal combustion engines. At present 97% of the energy used for U.S. vehicles derives from oil, with no other substitute on the horizon. Oil has proven itself a rocky investment medium, but overall it has been a solid performer, having increased in value more than tenfold over the past quarter century.

CRUDE OIL SPOT PRICE
ANNUALIZED RETURNS LESS INFLATION FOR VARIOUS FIVE YEAR PERIODS

Although oil's record for the past quarter century has been a good one, the gains came primarily in the 1970s. The past ten years, with the exception of 1987, 1989, and 1990, have all been losers. Oil was by far the most volatile of all investment groups monitored by the Chase Investment Performance Digest.

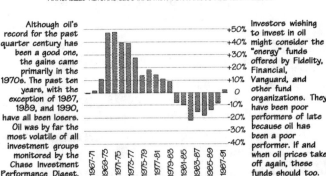

Investors wishing to invest in oil might consider the "energy" funds offered by Fidelity, Financial, Vanguard, and other fund organizations. They have been poor performers of late because oil has been a poor performer. If and when oil prices take off again, these funds should too.

Source: *Chase Investment Performance Digest.* 1992 Edition. © C. David Chase. All rights reserved. A product of Chase Global Data and Research, 289 Great Road, Acton, MA 01720. (508) 263-0404. Although gathered from reliable sources, data accuracy and completeness cannot be guaranteed.

Stock Market Basics

I. **Shares of stock represent part ownership in a business.**

   A. As an owner, you have the right to participate in the future growth of the company.

   B. You will receive dividends if the company decides to distribute money to shareholders rather than retain it for future growth needs.

   C. The other way you can profit is if the company grows and prospers; your ownership stake will grow in value as well.

II. **The stock market is where the buying and selling of part ownerships in businesses takes place.**

   A. Stock market prices rise and fall for the same reasons other prices do: from supply and demand forces that reflect economic conditions.

   B. Three major stock averages chart the price movements in the stock market.

   C. Ultimately, prices of stocks will reflect the underlying earnings and dividends of individual companies.

2

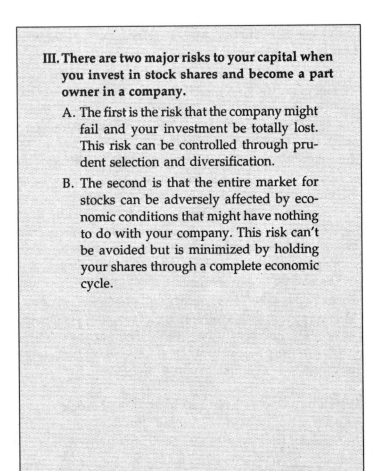

III. There are two major risks to your capital when you invest in stock shares and become a part owner in a company.

    A. The first is the risk that the company might fail and your investment be totally lost. This risk can be controlled through prudent selection and diversification.

    B. The second is that the entire market for stocks can be adversely affected by economic conditions that might have nothing to do with your company. This risk can't be avoided but is minimized by holding your shares through a complete economic cycle.

What we call "stocks" are actually pieces of paper that represent ownership in a company.

When corporations desire to raise money from investors for long-term working capital, they have two choices. One, they can borrow it by selling bonds. This approach means that the company will have to make regular interest payments to the bondholders, as well as pay all the money back some day. The investors play the role of lenders. Or two, the company can sell part ownerships in the company by offering *stock*. In that case, the investors play the role of owners. They are usually entitled to voting rights (which allow them to participate in electing the board of directors who oversee the running of the company, to vote on whether to merge with or sell to another company and under what terms, etc.) and they share in any dividends the board of directors may decide to pay out. However, they will not receive any interest payments on their investments (because they are owners, not lenders) and cannot necessarily count on ever getting their investment money back. Their fortunes are tied in with the future success or failure of the company.

When you decide to invest in shares of stock you've actually made a decision to "go into business." Just as with any business owner...

...you're last in line when it comes to dividing up the money that's (hopefully) pouring in from happy customers. Your company has to pay the suppliers that provide a variety of needed goods and supporting services. It has to buy equipment and then keep it well maintained. It has employees' salaries, related payroll taxes, health insurance, and retirement benefits to support. It needs to carry property, liability, and workman's compensation insurance. It regularly needs financial and legal services and must continually deal with government reporting requirements and other red tape.

Depending on the business, it might also need to invest large sums in product research and development, or massive sums for sales and marketing. And if it has borrowed any money for expansion or seasonal cash flow needs, it must pay the interest in full. Finally, if your company manages to pay all these bills and still has any money left over at year's end, governments at the local, state, and federal level all show up demanding a share of the profits.

All of this happens before you, the owner, receive a penny. Nobody said it would be easy.

Investors buy stock with the hope of profiting by either receiving dividends while they own the stock or by eventually selling their shares for more than they paid. Whatever money remains...

...at the very end, if any, is called the net profit. What you are hoping for is that (1) there will be some net profits every year, and (2) the net profits this year will be greater than the net profits last year. If these two things happen consistently—and despite the odds, they occasionally do—then you have a good chance of prospering along with the company.

For example, you might receive cash payments from the company as it distributes some of its accumulated profits to the owners—that's called dividend income. Or the board of directors might decide it's better to pay little or no dividends for the time being, preferring instead to keep the money to use for the additional expansion of the company. As the company's sales and profits grow over time, the price of its shares will hopefully gain in value as well—that's called capital growth. Dividend income and capital growth are the two primary rewards investors hope to receive in return for the risks they assume when they become shareholders in companies.

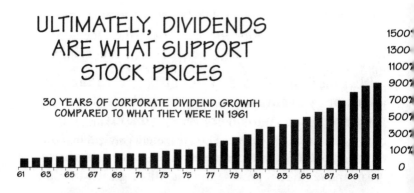

ULTIMATELY, DIVIDENDS ARE WHAT SUPPORT STOCK PRICES

30 YEARS OF CORPORATE DIVIDEND GROWTH
COMPARED TO WHAT THEY WERE IN 1961

1500%
1300
1100%
900%
700%
500%
300%
100%
0

61 63 65 67 69 71 73 75 77 79 81 83 85 87 89 91

Newcomers to stock investing are often confused as to what it is that makes the price of shares go up or down each day. Perhaps you've seen scenes of the stock trading activity at the New York Stock Exchange (NYSE) on the news and wondered what's going on down there. Well, "what's going on" is that thousands of investors worldwide have sent to buy and sell orders through their brokers for stocks listed on the NYSE, and they all collide on the floor in a kind of controlled chaos.

Come along, and I'll take you through a typical trade. Let's start by assuming that you own 100 shares of stock in Ford. As a shareholder...

...you are one of the owners of Ford Motor Company. Perhaps not a major owner, but an owner nevertheless. As a part-owner, you share in Ford's profits, if any. When Ford pays its shareholders a dividend, all the owners receive some money in proportion to how much of Ford they own.

As it happens, there are new people everyday who decide they, too, want to own stock in Ford. Perhaps they are portfolio managers who have extra money from investors to put to work and believe that Ford is the best value in the auto industry. Or, perhaps they are people who like the fact that Ford also pays an annual dividend of $1.60 per share. If they buy shares for $40 each, that $1.60 represents a yield of 4.0% on their money. For whatever reason, they want to buy shares in Ford.

It is also apparent each day that some of the current part owners of Ford decide they don't want to be part owners anymore. Let's say you're one of them. Perhaps you've decided that foreign imports are going to devastate American car makers, and you don't want to be in the automobile manufacturing business anymore. Or, maybe you still like Ford's competitive position in the industry but fear the economy is heading into a recession that will hurt Ford's profits and possibly cause Ford to reduce its $1.60 dividend. Or, maybe it has nothing to do with Ford or the economy; you just need the money for a down payment on a house, or for college tuition, or something else.

The point is you want to sell your shares in Ford. Now, where do you find all those new buyers I said were out there? For the most part...

...on the trading floor of the NYSE where people stand around all day long buying and selling part ownerships in companies. That's where your stockbroker comes in. All the major brokerage firms are members of the NYSE, and they have employees there whose job it is to carry out your orders.

So, you call your broker and tell him to sell your 100 shares immediately at the best price he can get. The order is sent to a floor worker, and when the market opens at 9:30 EST, he goes to the one place on the floor where Ford stock is traded. When he arrives, he encounters workers from other firms who are also carrying customer instructions to sell or buy Ford shares. On this particular morning, let's assume there are many more shares of Ford ready to be sold than there are to be purchased. In other words, the current supply of Ford stock for sale is greater than the demand for Ford stock at the current price. Although Ford last traded the day before at $40, it seems the most any buyer will offer this morning is $39. Since that's the best price available, your representative sells your shares at that price. Soon, "F 39" flashes across stock quotation machines all over the country, recording the fact that 100 shares of Ford (so well-known it is noted by the single-letter symbol F) just changed hands at $39 a share.

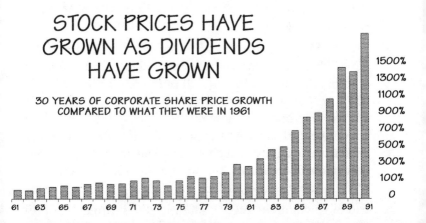

STOCK PRICES HAVE GROWN AS DIVIDENDS HAVE GROWN

30 YEARS OF CORPORATE SHARE PRICE GROWTH
COMPARED TO WHAT THEY WERE IN 1961

Who decided the price of Ford should drop that morning? The free market did—that is, the collective decisions of buyers and sellers (like you) from all over the world acting in their own self-interest made it happen. At the old price of $40, there were more shares of Ford to be sold than there were buyers for them; to attract more buyers, a lower price was necessary.

Throughout the day, every time Ford shares change hands, the number of shares and price will appear on the ticker tape. The price of the very last transaction of the day will appear in the next morning's paper as the "closing price." If that closing price is less than the previous day's closing price, then Ford will be said to have gone down that day.

What does it mean when we say that "the market was up" today?

Ford Motor is just one of more than 5,000 stocks for which daily price quotes are available. In order for the stock market to "go up," do all of them have to go up, or just a majority, or just a few of the important ones? To answer this question, market "averages" (or "indexes") were invented. Dozens of them are listed in *The Wall Street Journal* each day, but let's just look at three you should become familiar with.

The Dow Jones Industrial Average (DJIA) is the oldest and most widely quoted of all market indicators. It is prepared by Dow Jones & Company and is an average of the stock prices of thirty of the nation's strongest blue chip companies. The value of these companies represents 15%-20% of the total value of all the stocks that are traded on the New York Stock Exchange. Although the best known of the major averages, it is actually the least representative of daily market action.

The Standard & Poor's 500 Index (S&P 500) is published by Standard & Poor's, another giant financial news and information company. Composed of 500 stocks, it is more representative than the DJIA of what the overall market did on a certain day. As such, it is used by market professionals as the standard against which they compare their investment performance. It represents about 80% of the market value of all NYSE-traded stocks.

The Value Line Composite Index (VL 1700) is broader still. It includes *all* of the S&P 500 stocks plus a large number of smaller stocks traded over-the-counter. Maintained and published by the Value Line company, it represents *more than 95%* of the trading done each day in the U.S. markets. In our view, this comes closest of the three to measuring the extent to which "the market" is helping or hurting investors. Quite frequently, the DJIA and S&P 500 will show gains while the VL 1700 will fall. This means that although shares of the larger blue chips companies may have gone up, most stocks lost ground that day.

In our imaginary sale of Ford stock, we saw both of the major risks of owning a business come into play.

First, there's the risk that *the company you own* will fall on hard times. This is called the "business risk." In the example, this was manifested by concerns of sellers about the effects that foreign manufacturers are having on Ford's sales and profits. It could be due to poor management, labor-management conflicts, technological obsolescence, overwhelming

LOOK AT WHAT YOU DISCOVER WHEN YOU PUT DIVIDENDS AND STOCK PRICES TOGETHER

Combining the charts on pages 28 and 31, it becomes apparent that share prices (in shaded bars) have climbed much faster than dividends (solid bars) in recent years. Even the crash of 1987 didn't get the two back together as previous bear markets had done. Are the optimistically high prices of the late 1980s justified? This chart illustrates what commentators mean when they say, "The market has gotten ahead of itself." This should help you understand why it's reasonable to think stock prices might not go much higher than their 1991 levels until dividends can begin to catch up. In fact, the S&P 500 gained just 6.9% during the twenty-seven month period following the end of 1991.

competition, a shift in cultural behavior patterns, changing government policies, or any number of things. Considering all the things that can go wrong, it's a wonder that there are a large number of successful businesses. Separating the future winners from future losers requires knowledge, experience, wisdom, and a fair amount of good fortune. It is very difficult to do well on a consistent basis. If it were not, we'd all be making easy money in the stock market.

The second major risk of owning stocks is called the "market risk." This refers to those times when the stock market *as a whole* is being adversely effected by economic events. This takes place during the periodic recessions that the American economy goes through. In our example, it could be that Ford as a company is doing great, but lots of people still want to sell their Ford shares because they (1) fear a recession is coming and don't want to own any stocks, (2) have already been hurt by a recession and need to sell some of their stock to raise cash for living expenses, (3) have seen the recession drive down home prices and interest rates and are going to sell their stock in Ford to come up with the down payment money for a new house, and so on and so on.

As you can see, people often sell stock shares for reasons that have nothing directly to do with the prospects of the company. Many times, the sale of stock reflects the unfolding realities in the American and world economies and the level of interest rates. At other times selling takes place for purely emotional reasons. It has been said that "fear" and "greed" are the two primary forces that continually drive market activity. It's important to understand that ultimately your shares are worth what the market says they're worth, regardless of how seemingly well or poorly the company itself may be doing.

If you're beginning to think that the risks of owning stocks are considerable, that's good. You must...

...have a realistic view of this! The 1980s provided such a positive economic environment for stocks that many people have lost sight of the fact that stocks can lose value as well as gain it. Let's take a look at the historical record to put things into perspective. "Major Price Trends" (opposite page) shows stock price movements over the past thirty years. I have simplifed the chart by drawing in only the major price moves of 20% or more. The accompanying tables explain the letter codes on the graph, showing the amount of each move and how long it lasted. For example, the bull market indicated by the letters *A-B* gained 84% over a forty-four-month period.

Notice two key elements in the chart. First, the overall trend is up. Even the long sideways movement of the 1960s and 1970s had an upward bias. This upward trend reflects the underlying strength of American free-enterprise capitalism. As long as the economy is healthy and the population expanding, businesses have a favorable environment in which

MAJOR PRICE TRENDS IN THE STOCK MARKET

(Price moves of 20% or more as measured by the
Standard & Poor's 500 Stock Index from 1961-1991)

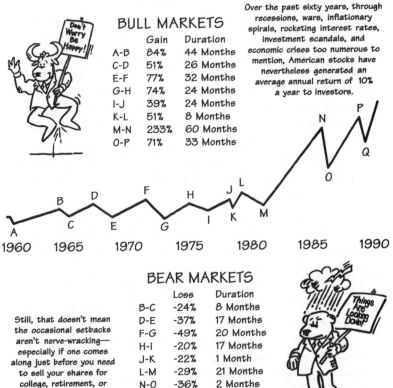

BULL MARKETS

	Gain	Duration
A-B	84%	44 Months
C-D	51%	26 Months
E-F	77%	32 Months
G-H	74%	24 Months
I-J	39%	24 Months
K-L	51%	8 Months
M-N	233%	60 Months
O-P	71%	33 Months

Over the past sixty years, through recessions, wars, inflationary spirals, rocketing interest rates, investment scandals, and economic crises too numerous to mention, American stocks have nevertheless generated an average annual return of 10% a year to investors.

1960   1965   1970   1975   1980   1985   1990

BEAR MARKETS

	Loss	Duration
B-C	-24%	8 Months
D-E	-37%	17 Months
F-G	-49%	20 Months
H-I	-20%	17 Months
J-K	-22%	1 Month
L-M	-29%	21 Months
N-O	-36%	2 Months
P-Q	-20%	3 Months

Still, that doesn't mean the occasional setbacks aren't nerve-wracking—especially if one comes along just before you need to sell your shares for college, retirement, or emergency needs.

they can prosper and grow. That means more profits. And more profits means more dividends being paid to the owners. Stock prices, ultimately, must reflect the earnings and dividends of the underlying companies.

Second, the last two bear markets were abrupt and relatively brief. This might be a reflection of the fact that the major financial markets are more global in nature than ever before. Americans are increasingly comfortable investing in Europe and Asia; overseas investors are major players in the American markets. With instantaneous communication of financial news, everyone trying to act on the same news at the same time creates a traffic jam. The markets aren't capable of handling the high volume of sales orders in stride. Large price markdowns are needed in order to entice a sufficient number of potential buyers off the sidelines.

To deal with these occasional bear markets, many investors use a strategy known as "market-timing" where they attempt to move out of stocks near market highs and buy back in near market lows. This has an appealing ring to it, but it has one disadvantage that is so troublesome that I have come to regard market-timing as unsuitable for the vast majority of investors. It's the human factor.

First, there's our natural greed. Peering blind-eyed into an impenetrable future, we hope for the best and talk ourselves into expecting the best. So if your trade turns into a loss and your timing system says to sell, you think, "Surely the market won't go straight down from here. There's bound to be at least a little bounce and I can get out without a loss." How many times have you decided to sell an investment "just as soon as the price gets back up to what I paid for it?"

Second, there's simple fear. Your system says "buy" but you're convinced by what you've been reading and hearing to expect further weakness instead. This causes you to lack confidence in your system's signal. You decide that if the market can prove itself by rising to Point X, *then* you'll buy. When Point X is reached, you feel better about the market's prospects, but you don't want to pay the higher price. Your plan becomes, "I'll buy on a pullback to Point Y." Assume you are given this second chance and Point Y is reached. Perversely, the very weakness that you were hoping for now causes you to doubt the authenticity of the rally. You again hesitate. While you're racked with indecision, the market roars off without looking back. When last seen, you were still trying to muster the courage to get invested.

The key to success is in being faithful. To be effective, even timing strategies require self-discipline. ◆

A Question of Value: Getting Your Money's Worth When Buying Stocks

I. **There are limits on what you should spend to buy a stock.**

   A. Apply value benchmarks to see if a stock is reasonably priced.

   B. There are historical norms that suggest a fair price for a company's stock in relation to its earnings, book value, and dividends.

II. **Investors in the stock market can be emotional as well as objective; that's why the markets do not always behave rationally.**

   A. The market is financially driven and therefore subject to many of the pressures of crowd psychology, including investors' false bravado, greed, and hysteria.

   B. Because of its susceptibility to crowd influences, stock prices at times can become overvalued (and undervalued). Long-term investors may need to be cautious about the timing of their initial investments.

3

III. The price-to-dividend ratio is a particularly useful indicator for determining the fair value for a share of stock.

   A. In the past, investors have typically valued the stocks in the Dow Industrials at around $24-$25 in price for every $1 they receive back in annual dividends.

   B. When they can "buy" $1 of dividends for $18 or less, they're getting a bargain; when they pay $29 or more, they're paying top dollar.

There are four words that give a lift to the spirit and encouragement to the body. They are words my family longs to hear...

...as we travel along life's highways. They conjure up warm feelings and happy memories. They have made such a difference in the way we think and plan that we can scarcely remember what life was like before we first learned them. Of course, I could only be referring to those four magical words: "Cracker Barrel. Next Exit."

I tell you this so you can fully appreciate that I really like the Cracker Barrel chain. Every time we travel, we invariably plan to catch lunch or dinner (and sometimes both!) at a Cracker Barrel restaurant. Even so, as much as my family values it, my enthusiasm has its limits. When I read in *Forbes* magazine recently that the chain earned $23 million in its last fiscal year, I was happy for the founders. But when I also read that investors were merrily paying around $35 per share to buy into this successful enterprise, I was aghast. Multiply that times the approximately 34 million shares outstanding, and you will discover the market is saying the company is worth about $1.2 billion!

Let me break that down into something more manageable for you. Let's say you're considering buying a restaurant business that is successful and growing. Last year, it earned $185,000 and could earn as much as $240,000 this year. If you could afford it, would you be willing to pay

$1 million to buy a business like that? Sure, because you could recoup your investment in three to four years at the rate the business is growing. Well, how about paying $2 million? Still a good deal. How about $4 million? Hmmm... well, possibly. Now it might take as long as sixteen years, depending on how well future growth develops, to get your initial investment back.

OK, how about $6 million? At this point, it's getting expensive. The purchase price represents twenty-four times this year's expected profits. Over twenty-four years, there's a much greater risk that unanticipated events could limit growth plans. So maybe, maybe not. It depends how badly you want to own this business. How about $8 million? No, now the seller has gone too far. As great as you think the business is, no way it's worth that much. How about $9.6 million? Good grief, no! Who would want to pay a price equal to forty times this year's expected earnings to purchase a business? Well, that's what buyers of Cracker Barrel stock at $35 a share are doing.

Investors can often justify paying a high asking price if: (1) they believe the growth prospects of a company are outstanding enough; (2) they are optimistic about the American economy; and (3) they are patient and willing to take a very long-term view. Such optimism is usually the result of projecting the current favorable trends almost indefinitely into the future. Of course, this ignores the limitations of human understanding and the uncertainty of future developments.

You shouldn't expect the markets to always behave rationally.

Because the financial markets constantly speak a language of numbers, we get the impression that investing is like scientific research—when you add up all the proven facts, you can arrive at the "correct" answer. We assume there are objective rules that should govern our decision-making—that investing decisions can be made with mathematical certainty.

None of this is the case. Investing is more of an art than a science. There are very few rules, and decision making is almost entirely subjective. The markets are merely collections of people who act according to their emotions and desires of the moment. We've all observed (and probably contributed to) how people act differently when they are part of a crowd than when they are acting alone. Gustave Le Bon wrote his classic study of "crowd psychology" in 1895, but it's always been a part of human nature—from the behavior of Joseph's brothers thousands of years ago to the L.A. riots of 1992. We see people exhibiting false bravado, greed, and hysteria when they are part of a group that they would be quite unlikely to show as individuals acting alone. Peer pressure also plays a major role. In the same way, the herd mentality in the stock market often leads investors to actions they later regret.

Fifty years before Le Bon's work, an Englishman named Charles Mackay became interested in the psychological aspects of crowd behavior with respect to people's investment decisions. After analyzing several early widespread financial manias (such as the Dutch Tulipmania and the South Sea Bubble), he wrote a book that has become a classic: *Extraordinary Popular Delusions and the Madness of Crowds*. When you hear the details of these infamous financial episodes, it's hard to believe that otherwise rational people could get so caught up in a mass delusion. After these bubbles burst, the participants themselves are hard pressed to explain their own behavior. Although published in 1841, the lessons it teaches are still instructive today. Because of human nature and our susceptibility to crowd influences, it isn't unusual for markets and stock prices to become overvalued (or undervalued) for brief periods of time.

Should this matter to long-term investors? If you're willing to invest in stocks and maintain your commitments over the long haul (ten to fifteen years), does it really make a difference if you pay a little too much at the outset? The answer to that depends on how much is "too much" and what the following decade is like. Consider the fate of investors during the early 1970s who didn't mind paying top dollar for shares in quality companies.

After the crash of the high-flying stocks of the 1960s, money managers made a dramatic turn toward quality. No more speculative stuff...

...only the best would do. They sought out blue chip companies with proven growth records. Four dozen or so companies soon became regarded as the premier growth stocks of the day. The list included familiar names such as IBM, Xerox, Kodak, Disney, Polaroid, and Avon. They became known as the "Nifty Fifty" and were thought to be stocks that could be bought and—due to their stature, profitability, and future prospects—held virtually for a lifetime if investors so wished. And since you had such a long-term view, what did it matter if the price you paid per share was on the expensive side? *Forbes* magazine said, "The delusion was that these companies were so good that it didn't matter what you paid for them; their inexorable growth would bail you out."

It seemed everyone wanted to own these same high-quality stocks. The prices kept going higher and higher, but the buyers kept coming. In fact, the more the prices pushed higher, the more it seemed to validate the excellence of the Nifty Fifty. By late 1972, these stocks were selling for prices that could not be justified by the earnings and future prospects of the companies. Eventually, of course, the mania for the Nifty Fifty ended. It ended as all bubbles do—when demand was finally exhausted. This occurred when the last buyer who just "had" to own the Nifty Fifty satisfied his desire. After that, the only investors left were those who, although they might admire the quality of the Nifty Fifty companies, were unwilling to pay exorbitant prices.

POPULAR BENCHMARKS USEFUL FOR DECIDING IF A STOCK IS REASONABLY PRICED

The Price-to-Earning Ratio (P/E)

This ratio is calculated by dividing the price of a stock by its reported earnings for the past four quarters. If your favorite stock, Can't Miss, Inc., is selling for $40 a share and has reported earnings for the past twelve months of $2 per share, it is said to have a P/E of 20 ($40/$2). The problem with using earnings as a guide to stock valuation is they are very susceptible to manipulation by the company. Accounting principles and I.R.S. rules offer a variety of ways to deal with depreciation, research expenses, marketing expenses, inventory costs, and so on. A company can postpone reporting "bad news" through the creative use of accounting. Other problems with using earnings include: The P/E becomes abnormally high when earnings drop to a low level, and the tendency is to justify higher prices by using projected future earnings rather than current earnings when computing the P/E.

The Price-to-Book Ratio (P/B)

This approach relies on the size of a company's assets (rather than its earning power) to determine its share value. The book value is theoretically what you get if you were to sell all the company's assets, pay off all its liabilities, and pay what's left to the shareholders. If Can't Miss, Inc., has a book value of $10 per share, it's P/B is 4.0 ($40/$10). This ratio suffers from the same failing as the P/E: It's highly subject to variation depending upon the accounting practices of the company. The actual value of the company assets might be much higher than reported (for example, if land owned in downtown Dallas is carried on the books at the low price paid for the land thirty years ago), or much lower than reported (for example, deferred expenses for research are carried on the books of the company as having value when in fact the research proved fruitless).

The Price-to-Dividends Ratio (P/D)

Only the price-to-dividend ratio reflects the actual reality experienced by shareholders. The reported earning per share or book value per share may be subject to manipulation by the company, but there is no doubt surrounding the amount of dividends it is paying out. Either you received dividends in a certain amount, or you didn't. If you received $1.60 per share, then the P/D ratio is 25 ($40/$1.60).

At that point, prices can only go in one direction: down. Let me use the story of the Mazda Miata...

...to illustrate why it must be this way. In 1990, Mazda's new two-seater sports convertible hit the market and received rave reviews. Dealers found that because interest in this new car was so intense and supplies were still limited, they could charge more than the $16,000 sticker price and still sell all they could get their hands on. There were reports of consumers paying a dealer $18,000 and immediately selling the car to another eager buyer for a quick profit. As Miata-mania grew, the cars were changing hands for as much as $30,000 and more. The buyers were people who just "had" to have one—even if it meant paying absolutely top dollar.

As you might expect, there is only a limited number of such carefree spenders (even among fad-conscious, buy-now-and-pay-later baby boomers). When the last determined buyer finally acquired his Miata, the upward pressure on prices disappeared. So, when the next Miata owner decided to sell—because the novelty of cramped, noisy, and rough-riding transportation had worn off—there was no one left who would pay $30,000. There were still people who would like to own one, but not for $30,000! To attract a buyer, sellers needed to drop the asking price until someone was enticed off the sidelines. The balance of power then shifted from the sellers to the buyers. Once this happened, it was only a matter of time before the price returned to its former fair value range. Two years later, you could buy a 1990 Miata for $12,000-$13,000.

With similar forces at work on the Nifty Fifty, prices began to plunge in the beginning of 1973. When the dust settled eighteen months later, the Standard & Poor's 500 Stock Index had fallen 45% in price. Many of the Nifty Fifty did much worse (for example, Avon and Polaroid fell an amazing 87% and 91% respectively). Many highly respected stock mutual funds also fell dramatically from their 1972 highs. Imagine Magellan dropping 59%, Mathers 56%, Nicholas 69%, Price New Horizons 64%, 20th Century Growth 46%, and Explorer Fund 52%! Eventually the funds would rise back to their former heights, but many investors couldn't endure the uncertainty of a long wait and sold at a loss. For those who stuck it out, twelve long years went by before they caught up with those cautious souls who had resisted the lure of the Nifty Fifty in the first place and remained in treasury bills the entire time. Obviously, even for long-term investors there's a limit to what is a reasonable price to pay for stock shares.

How, then, can you calculate the "fair" value for a share of stock?

That's a difficult question. Since a share of stock makes you a part owner in a business, it's actually the same as asking how to calculate the value of a business. There are specialists who spend years learning how to do this, and even then their conclusions are merely expressions of their training, opinions, and biases. Common sense says the value should have something to do with the (1) assets owned by the business, (2) level

APPLYING VALUE BENCHMARKS TO THE STOCK MARKET

When you see the price-to-dividend ratio of the Dow and S&P 500 above $29, you know stocks generally are overpriced. When you see the ratio at $34 or higher, it indicates that stocks have outpaced dividends and have relatively little further upside potential until earnings and dividends can catch up.

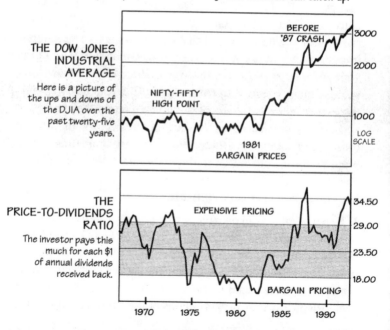

THE DOW JONES INDUSTRIAL AVERAGE

Here is a picture of the ups and downs of the DJIA over the past twenty-five years.

BEFORE '87 CRASH — 3000

2000

NIFTY-FIFTY HIGH POINT

1000

LOG SCALE

1981 BARGAIN PRICES

THE PRICE-TO-DIVIDENDS RATIO

The investor pays this much for each $1 of annual dividends received back.

EXPENSIVE PRICING — 34.50

29.00

23.50

18.00

BARGAIN PRICING

1970   1975   1980   1985   1990

of annual profits earned, and (3) dividends paid to shareholders. But adding to the difficulty is the fact that projections about profits must be made for many years into the future.

When assessing the stock market *as a whole,* a benchmark that I rely on heavily is the level of dividends paid to shareholders each year. At the left, there is a graph of the price movement of the Dow Jones Industrials Average over the past quarter century. Directly under it, I have placed a second graph. It charts the historical relationship between stock prices and the dividends received by investors. Called the "price-to-dividends ratio," it shows how much investors pay in price for each $1 of annual dividends they receive back. *The p/d is computed by dividing the current price by the dividends received by shareholders over the past 12 months.* Historically, the ratio has been between 18 and 29 roughly one-half the time (the shaded area or "fair value" range of the chart). One-fourth of the time it is below 18 (bargain time!), and one-fourth of the time it is above 29 (relatively expensive). You can see the different results that follow from buying at bargain prices versus paying top dollar.

Excursions into expensive territory are usually brief. The ratio returns to the fair value area as prices fall, dividends rise, or a combination of both take place. A research project published in the *Stock Market Logic* newsletter showed how the S&P 500 performed in the past once the p/d ratio reached an extreme reading of $34. On average, the overall market was 5% lower one year later and 10% lower two years later. Historically, investors have seen the value of their shares fall during the first two years when buying at overvalued levels.

These tendencies apply to the stock market as a whole. Naturally, there are always some stocks that can be purchased at reasonable valuations even when the overall market is over-priced—that's why "value" investors can continue to find bargains. But since you will primarily be using mutual funds, which tend to move with the overall market (due to their broad diversification), it's essential that you understand the significance of these valuation benchmarks and what they tell us about the current level of risk.

Removing your money from the safety of savings accounts and CDs in order to invest in the market...

...is always a risky thing to do. Don't let low interest rates on your savings tempt you to invest money in stocks unless you can afford to take a much greater risk. Just because stocks are going up doesn't mean they're a good buy or that they will continue to rise. The relationship between price and dividends eventually reasserts itself. Keep an eye on value. For the past quarter century (other than in 1972 during the heyday of the Nifty Fifty), investors have had an opportunity *at some point during each and every year* to buy blue chip stocks in the fair value range *if* they were suffi-ciently patient. Be patient. ◆

SECTOR FUNDS: HANDLE WITH CARE

Sector funds specialize in just one industry (or sector) of our economy, such as banking and financial services, health care, high-tech, or precious metals. They often attract attention because they can turn in excellent performance if "their" sector of the economy is growing rapidly. The trade-off, however, is a much higher degree of risk due to their lack of industry diversification. That's why only experienced investors should consider sector funds for inclusion in their portfolios.

The table below shows six of the sectors most popular with fund investors. You can see from the wide range of the performance numbers (for the five year period ending 6/30/92) that there is a great deal of difference in results, even among funds investing in the same sectors.

	Financial Services	Health Related	Precious Metals	Natural Resources	High Technology	Utilities
Number of Funds	9	10	32	20	17	23
Average Size (In Millions)	$70	$529	$80	$86	$105	$497
Average Expense Ratio	1.75	1.47	1.96	2.16	1.35	1.29
Average Portfolio Turnover	122%	94%	58%	111%	136%	48%
Average Return Past 5 Yrs	12.8%	15.4%	-6.9%	2.2%	5.2%	9.9%
Best Fund In Group	18.9%	23.4%	6.8%	7.5%	11.6%	13.8%
Worst Fund In Group	2.2%	6.8%	-24.2%	-5.7%	0.9%	-3.9%
A No-Load Fund Worth Investigating	Financial Strategic Fin Serv	Financial Strategic Health Serv	Vanguard Specialized Gold	Price New Era Fund	Financial Strategic Technology	Financial Strategic Utilities
Telephone:1-800	525-8085	525-8085	662-7447	638-5660	525-8085	525-8085

4

How to Shop for Stock Funds

I. When assessing risk, knowing the investing "style" used by the fund and the average size of the companies in which it invests provides helpful guidance.

   A. Two of the major styles of investing are *value* and *growth*. The value approach is the more conservative because of its emphasis on getting your money's worth.

   B. *Large* companies are generally safer to invest in than *small* companies although they don't have the capital gain potential.

II. By categorizing funds according to their actual portfolio holdings, we can create a helpful guide to risk using the characteristics of *value* versus *growth* and *large* versus *small* companies.

   A. The funds with the lowest risk/reward characteristics will be those that follow a value/large company strategy.

   B. The highest risk/reward potential is found among funds that employ a growth/small company strategy.

C. The risk profile concept illustrates the way these four characteristics interact.

III. We take a look at the historical performance of the four different risk profile categories.

A. Each of the four categories is reviewed in terms of its historic performance results, volatility, and ability to outpace inflation.

B. In each category, four no-load funds are listed as being worthy of consideration; performance data and portfolio character-istics are provided for each.

It has been my experience that the mutual fund industry categorizes stock-oriented funds in a confusing way that offers little practical guidance to the average investor.

Take the definitions offered by the Investment Company Institute (at far right), the industry trade association and the one group from whom you'd expect the clearest set of guidelines for categorizing funds according to their risk and suitability. The list is really nothing more than the most commonly stated portfolio objectives as found in a fund prospectus. The problem with this is that these are often little more than general statements of theoretical goals and strategies; a fund's actual portfolio risk has tremendous room for variance while still staying within the broad guidelines given.

What you're looking for is an indication of the road the fund is traveling in terms of risk and possible reward. If you saw your neighbor loading up the car for a trip and asked him where he was going, you wouldn't learn very much if all he said was "somewhere warm." That would eliminate a lot of places he *wouldn't* be going, but it really wouldn't pinpoint where he *was* going. That's also true of the way many mutual funds state their objectives. They tell you generally what they are allowed to do and not do, but beyond that a lot is uncertain. In fact, the very fact that there are no "official" categories everyone can agree upon proves how subjective risk-assessment is.

I will use a different approach that classifies stock funds by a criteria that I believe should be of greater interest to investors—one that recognizes the actual investment strategy currently being used by the fund manager. For the most part, investing strategies (or "styles") used by portfolio managers of stock funds can be grouped into two major camps. First, there is the *value* camp, which emphasizes how much you're getting for your investment dollar. This kind of manager primarily considers the present state of a company's assets, earnings, and dividends in arriving at an assessment of its stock's intrinsic value. They prefer to bargain-hunt, and they often end up buying unglamorous, unappreciated companies (because that's where the bargains are). Value managers are serious about getting their money's worth. If a bear market comes along, they shouldn't get hurt too badly because many of the

THE MAJOR CLASSIFICATIONS FOR STOCK FUNDS

AS ISSUED BY THE INVESTMENT COMPANY INSTITUTE

Aggressive Growth Funds

Seek maximum capital gains. Some may invest in stocks of businesses that are somewhat out of the mainstream, and may also use specialized investing techniques such as option-writing, short-selling and short-term trading.

Growth Funds

invest in the common stocks of well-established companies. Their primary aim is to produce an increase in the value of their investments (capital gains) rather than a flow of dividends.

Growth & Income Funds

invest mainly in the common stock of companies that have had increasing share value but also a solid record of paying dividends. This type of fund attempts to combine long-term capital growth with a steady stream of income.

Equity Income Funds

Seek a high level of current income by investing in equity securities of companies with good dividend-paying records.

stocks they buy have already been beaten down in price (which is when *they* bought them) and hopefully wouldn't fall much further. The drawback is that the reason a stock is bargain priced in the first place is that it either has operating problems or is simply out of favor with investors. It often takes *years* for such stock purchases to bear fruit. It requires p-a-t-i-e-n-c-e to be a value investor.

The other style of stock investing is the *growth* camp. The managers with this strategy act on future expectations. They would say, "Look at all the great things the company has going for it! It has a tremendous future ahead." A great deal of their success hinges on the ability to accurately predict corporate earnings a few years into the future. When measured in terms of the company's current earnings and dividends, the stock may appear expensive at present, but if the company can achieve its potential, today's share price will look like a bargain a few years from now. When they're right in their projections and they've got a good economy to work with, they can hit home runs. But this approach carries more risk because growth stocks typically *are already priced* on the assumption that all the future good news will come to pass. As we saw in our look at the Nifty Fifty earlier, if there are disappointments along the way, the share prices of growth stocks have a lot of room to fall.

Historically, both kinds of investment philosophies have made money, but no investment style results in top performance year after year. As we go through the recurring growth-recession cycle, economic events favor different styles at different times. Although "value" funds tend to have the best long-term records, they can still underperform for long periods at a time. Windsor Fund, Mutual Shares, and Lindner Fund were all top performers in the mid-1980s only to fall to the bottom 25% of stock funds over the past three to five years.

The point is not necessarily to try to pick one style over the other—both will have their "day in the sun" at various times. In fact, structuring your portfolio so as to include stock funds using each philosophy is a sensible diversification move.

Let's develop a risk profile. First, we'll divide a large diamond into four smaller diamond-shaped compartments. The idea is to place all stock funds into one of the four compartments using criteria that we feel have the greatest

BUILDING A RISK PROFILE FOR STOCK FUNDS: STEP #1

First, we divide the diamond to show the two major investing styles.

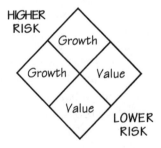

Funds will be placed in either the growth or value half of the profile depending on the investing strategy being reflected in the fund's current portfolio.

BUILDING A RISK PROFILE FOR STOCK FUNDS: STEP #2

Next, we factor in the risk of investing in small companies vs. large companies.

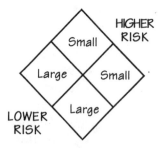

Stock funds will be placed in either the "small" or "large" sections of the profile depending on the average size of the companies whose stock is owned in the portfolios.

bearing on risk. In this way, we can get a quick insight into the general riskiness of a fund just by seeing in which of the four compartments it is placed.

Along one side of the diamond, we'll put the investing styles of value and growth (see step #1 graphic on page 59). As we've discussed, a value style generally has less risk than a growth style because of the emphasis on buying at bargain prices and holding for the long haul. How are you to know which style of investing a particular fund is following? In a recent report, *Morningstar Mutual Funds* suggested using a fund's current price/earnings and price/book ratios (which you can obtain from the fund with a phone call) as a guide.

Since valuation is relative, the fund's ratios should be compared to benchmark ratios like those of the S&P 500 in order to be more meaningful. Morningstar used these ratios to assign every fund to one of three different style categories: value, growth, and a combination of the two. I've adapted this concept to our risk diamond approach by eliminating the "combination" category. This makes the guidelines somewhat less precise but gains in simplicity and ease of use. Here is how it works.

In step 2 (far left), we contrast buying large companies with buying small companies. Larger companies, like those in the Dow Jones Industrial Average and the S&P 500 Stock Index, are usually stronger in terms of market penetration and financial strength. Their earnings might be temporarily affected by competitive pressures, technological developments, or a recession, but they are expected to survive and prosper. Smaller companies carry higher risk because they are more easily devastated by such setbacks. On the other hand, they have the potential to grow to ten, twenty, or fifty times their present size. The time to "get in on the ground floor" is when they're still small. Deciding exactly when a company moves from the small to the large category is strictly a matter of opinion. For our purposes here, if a company's market capitalization (that is, the total market value of all the company's outstanding stock) is under $2 billion, I'll treat it as a small company; over $2 billion and I put it in the large company category.

Now look at what happens when we put it all together (graph on next page). We now have four distinct types of

BUILDING A RISK PROFILE FOR STOCK FUNDS: STEP #3

Now we can assign each of 528 stock funds to one of the four risk diamonds depending upon their current portfolio holdings. A fund's risk category can change if its portfolio holdings change sufficiently; the numbers below reflect an analysis done in 1992.

The lowest-risk funds are found in diamond ❶, the next lowest in diamond ❷, and so on.

fund portfolios from which we can choose with some degree of confidence that we understand the investment strategy and risk of loss associated with each. As you can see, the
risk is lowest at the bottom of the profile and greatest at the
top. On the following pages, we'll look at historical performance data and recommended funds from each of these four
groups.

One last point. Bear in mind that I assigned each fund to
one of the four groups based on its actual portfolio holdings
using the most current information available. Mutual fund
portfolios change on a daily basis. The portfolio information
is dated by the time it gets to me and even more so by the
time you read this book. But you can contact the funds in
which you're interested and get up-to-the-minute information. If a fund has made a major shift in its strategy, it should
become apparent when you are comparing the new information with what appears in the following tables. ◆

The Characteristics of a Large-Company / Value Strategy

Invests primarily in established companies which are leaders in their industries. This lowers risk.

Commitment to buying only at bargain prices caused by temporary market factors. This lowers risk.

This is the most conservative of the four strategies in our risk profile for stock funds. As you move through this section, you will notice the graphs show greater ups and downs as risk increases.

REPRESENTATIVE OF THIS GROUP IS THE

NEUBERGER/BERMAN GUARDIAN

ANNUALIZED RETURNS FOR VARIOUS TWELVE-MONTH PERIODS

Most performance graphs you see in the financial media show one year returns only from January through December. That doesn't really give you a clear picture of the volatility you can expect because investors don't buy only on January 2 and sell only on December 31.

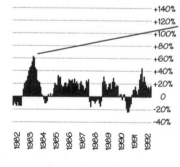

These graphs show one year performance no matter which month you begin. Each of the bars represents a different twelve-month period. For example, the tallest one shows the period from mid-1982 to mid-1983 when the Guardian fund returned over 60% to shareholders.

Source: *Morningstar Mutual Funds OnDisc* © Morningstar, Inc. 53 West Jackson Blvd., Chicago, IL 60604. (800) 876-5005. Although gathered from reliable sources, data accuracy and completeness cannot be guaranteed. Contact the fund for current information before you invest.

Recent Performance Results of a Large-Company / Value Strategy

Average Annual Return for 1991-1993 Period for the Funds in This Category +16.8% Per Year	Average Annual "Real" Return for 1991-1993 Period for the Funds in This Category +13.2% Per Year

No-Load Funds in This Category You Might Consider	Fidelity Equtiy Income II	Babson Value	Dremen High-Return	Fidelity Stock Selector
Morningstar Risk Category	Equity Income	Growth & Income	Growth & Income	Growth
Avg Return Past 3 Years	27.6%	22.3%	24.6%	24.3%
Total Return for 1993	18.9%	22.9%	9.4%	14.0%
Total Return for 1992	19.1%	15.4%	19.8%	15.4%
Total Return for 1991	46.6%	28.9%	47.6%	45.9%
Total Return for 1990	new	-11.4%	-8.6%	new
Total Return for 1989	new	18.2%	18.5%	new
Minimum Purchase	$2,500	$1,000	$1,000	$2,500
Toll Free: Call 1-800	544-8888	422-2766	533-1608	544-8888
Nasdaq Ticker Symbol	FEQTX	BVALX	DRHRX	FDSSX

Footnote: The Avg Return Past 3 Years is the annualized rate for the period 1/1/91-12/31/93. By the time you read this, these funds may have characteristics different from those shown. These are not recommended funds per se, but are offered here as worthy of consideration.

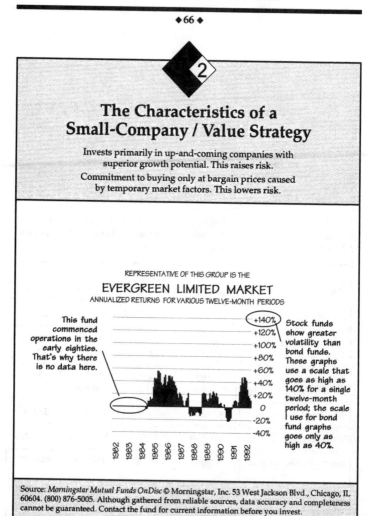

2

The Characteristics of a Small-Company / Value Strategy

Invests primarily in up-and-coming companies with superior growth potential. This raises risk.

Commitment to buying only at bargain prices caused by temporary market factors. This lowers risk.

REPRESENTATIVE OF THIS GROUP IS THE

EVERGREEN LIMITED MARKET

ANNUALIZED RETURNS FOR VARIOUS TWELVE-MONTH PERIODS

This fund commenced operations in the early eighties. That's why there is no data here.

+140%
+120%
+100%
+80%
+60%
+40%
+20%
0
-20%
-40%

1982 1983 1984 1985 1986 1987 1988 1989 1990 1991 1992

Stock funds show greater volatility than bond funds. These graphs use a scale that goes as high as 140% for a single twelve-month period; the scale I use for bond fund graphs goes only as high as 40%.

Source: *Morningstar Mutual Funds OnDisc* © Morningstar, Inc. 53 West Jackson Blvd., Chicago, IL 60604. (800) 876-5005. Although gathered from reliable sources, data accuracy and completeness cannot be guaranteed. Contact the fund for current information before you invest.

Recent Performance Results of a Small-Company / Value Strategy

Average Annual Return for 1991-1993 Period for the Funds in This Category +22.2% Per Year	Average Annual "Real" Return for 1991-1993 Period for the Funds in This Category +18.6% Per Year

No-Load Funds in This Category You Might Consider	Babson Enterprise	Evergreen Limited Market	Price Small Cap. Value	Mutual Beacon
Morningstar Risk Category	Small Company	Small Company	Small Company	Growth & Income
Avg Return Past 3 Years	27.5%	22.2%	26.0%	21.1%
Total Return for 1993	16.3%	9.6%	23.3%	22.9%
Total Return for 1992	24.6%	10.1%	20.9%	22.9%
Total Return for 1991	43.0%	51.1%	34.2%	17.6%
Total Return for 1990	-15.9%	-10.4%	-11.3%	-8.2%
Total Return for 1989	22.5%	20.9%	18.1%	17.5%
Minimum Purchase	Closed	$5,000	$2,500	$5,000
Toll Free: Call 1-800	422-2766	235-0064	638-5660	553-3014
Nasdaq Ticker Symbol	BABEX	EVLMX	PRSVX	BEGRX

Footnote: The Avg Return Past 3 Years is the annualized rate for the period 1/1/91-12/31/93. By the time you read this, these funds may have characteristics different from those shown. These are not recommended funds per se, but are offered here as worthy of consideration.

The Characteristics of a Large-Company / Growth Strategy

Invests primarily in established companies which are leaders in their industries. This lowers risk.

Willingness to pay more for companies with above-average growth potential. This raises risk.

Turn back to page 64, and compare that graph to this one. Both funds invest in larger, well-established companies, but the difference between the value and growth strategies used by the two funds makes a world of difference in their risk and volatility.

REPRESENTATIVE OF THIS GROUP IS THE

20TH CENTURY GROWTH FUND
ANNUALIZED RETURNS FOR VARIOUS TWELVE-MONTH PERIODS

Consider this period when the fund showed gains of over 80% for a single twelve-month period, only to be followed by a loss of 25% a year later. Compare how this differs from the Guardian graph on page 64.

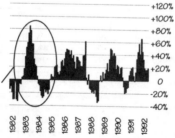

On this page (and on page 70) we see two funds managed by 20th Century Investors, one of the best no-load organizations around if exciting market movements are what you're looking for!

Source: *Morningstar Mutual Funds OnDisc* © Morningstar, Inc. 53 West Jackson Blvd., Chicago, IL 60604. (800) 876-5005. Although gathered from reliable sources, data accuracy and completeness cannot be guaranteed. Contact the fund for current information before you invest.

3

Recent Performance Results of a Large-Company / Growth Strategy

Average Annual Return
for 1991-1993 Period for
the Funds in This Category
+17.6% Per Year

Average Annual "Real" Return
for 1991-1993 Period for
the Funds in This Category
+14.0% Per Year

No-Load Funds in This Category You Might Consider	Founders Growth	Harbor Capital Apprec.	Strong Total Return	Neuberger/ Berman Manhattan
Morningstar Risk Category	Growth	Growth	Growth & Income	Growth
Avg Return Past 3 Years	24.5%	24.0%	18.1%	19.3%
Total Return for 1993	25.5%	12.1%	22.5%	10.0%
Total Return for 1992	4.3%	10.0%	0.6%	17.8%
Total Return for 1991	47.4%	54.8%	33.6%	30.9%
Total Return for 1990	-10.6%	-1.8%	-7.1%	-8.1%
Total Return for 1989	41.7%	24.2%	2.6%	29.1%
Minimum Purchase	$1,000	$2,000	$250	$1,000
Toll Free: Call 1-800	525-2440	422-1050	368-1030	877-9700
Nasdaq Ticker Symbol	FRGRX	HACAX	STRFX	NMANX

Footnote: The Avg Return Past 3 Years is the annualized rate for the period 1/1/91-12/31/93. By the time you read this, these funds may have characteristics different from those shown. These are not recommended funds per se, but are offered here as worthy of consideration.

The Characteristics of a Small-Company / Growth Strategy

Invests primarily in up-and-coming companies with superior growth potential. This raises risk.

Willingness to pay more for companies with above-average growth potential. This raises risk.

This is about as wild as it gets; this fund is not for the faint of heart!

REPRESENTATIVE OF THIS GROUP IS THE

20TH CENTURY ULTRA FUND

ANNUALIZED RETURNS FOR VARIOUS TWELVE-MONTH PERIODS

Some investors look at a graph like this and only "see" the times they could have doubled their money (and more) in a single twelve-month period. But don't pass too quickly over these down periods— they can be very tough to endure emotionally.

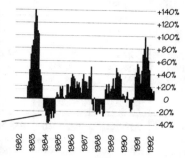

This fund is exceptionally volatile. The average fund in this group, although high in risk, would not show ups and downs as dramatic as these.

Source: *Morningstar Mutual Funds OnDisc* © Morningstar, Inc. 53 West Jackson Blvd., Chicago, IL 60604. (800) 876-5005. Although gathered from reliable sources, data accuracy and completeness cannot be guaranteed. Contact the fund for current information before you invest.

Recent Performance Results of a Small-Company / Growth Strategy

Average Annual Return for 1991-1993 Period for the Funds in This Category +25.4% Per Year	Average Annual "Real" Return for 1991-1993 Period for the Funds in This Category +21.8% Per Year

No-Load Funds in This Category You Might Consider	Kaufman	20th Century Ultra	Price New Horizons	SteinRoe Capital Oppor.
Morningstar Risk Category	Aggressive Growth	Small Company	Small Company	Aggressive Growth
Avg Return Past 3 Years	33.2%	32.0%	27.1%	28.6%
Total Return for 1993	18.2%	21.8%	22.0%	27.5%
Total Return for 1992	11.3%	1.3%	10.6%	2.4%
Total Return for 1991	79.4%	86.5%	52.2%	62.8%
Total Return for 1990	-6.1%	9.4%	-9.5%	-29.1%
Total Return for 1989	46.9%	36.9%	26.2%	36.8%
Minimum Purchase	$1,500	$1,000	$2,500	$1,000
Toll Free: Call 1-800	237-0132	345-2021	638-5660	338-2550
Nasdaq Ticker Symbol	KAUFX	TWCUX	PRNHX	SRFCX

Footnote: The Avg Return Past 3 Years is the annualized rate for the period 1/1/91-12/31/93. By the time you read this, these funds may have characteristics different from those shown. These are not recommended funds per se, but are offered here as worthy of consideration.

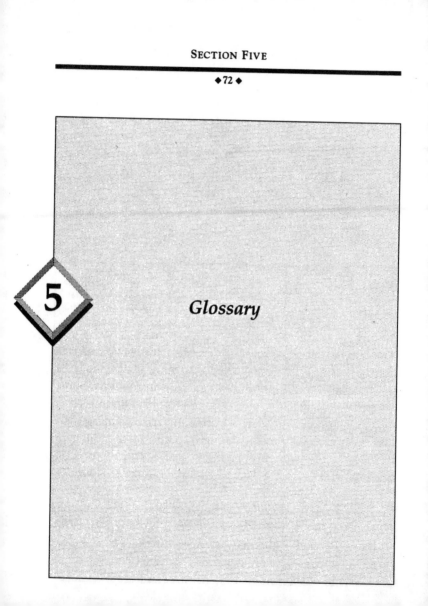

5 *Glossary*

Annual Report

is a report issued to shareholders, required by the Securities and Exchange Commission, that includes financial statements, a description of the company's operations over the past year, and management's assessment of its future prospects.

Blue Chip Stocks

are shares of large, well-known companies that have long records of profit growth, dividend payments, and reputations for quality products or services.

Bull and Bear Markets

are investment terms that date back to the California gold rush of 1848 when miners would entertain themselves with bullfights. To add variety, they began pitting the bulls against the powerful grizzlies that roamed wild in the area. Sometimes the bull would win by impaling the bear and tossing it *up* over his shoulder. But more often the grizzly emerged the victor by using its massive strength to wrestle the bull *down* to the ground, frequently breaking its neck in the process. The bull won by taking its opponent up, but the bear won by taking its opponent down. The terms were later introduced in San Francisco, where active trading took place in mining shares, to describe opposing investors who fought to establish the direction of the market. Accordingly, a bull market is one in which prices are generally rising while a bear market is one in which prices are generally falling.

Closing Price
is the price at which a security last traded before the close of business on a given day.

Common Stock
are the units of ownership in a corporation.

Dividends
are payments to shareholders as their share of the profits. They are usually made quarterly and are taxable in the year they are received.

Dollar-Cost-Averaging
is a strategy that spreads risk by investing a set dollar amount on a regular schedule (e.g., $50 a month). By keeping the investment amount constant, more shares of the security are purchased when prices are low than when prices are high.

Dow Jones Industrial Average
dates back to 1884 when Charles Dow first came up with the idea of using a small group of stocks to represent the market as a whole. He first selected only eleven stocks, but the average was expanded to its present number of thirty stocks in 1928 in order to better reflect the breadth of the American economy. Although the Dow is the world's best known stock average, its accuracy as a market barometer is limited because it reflects such a small number of companies.

Gold Standard

is a monetary system under which units of currency, in our case dollars, are convertible into fixed amounts of gold. That means for every dollar printed and put into circulation, the U.S. government theoretically has gold in storage to back it up (in case someone wants to exchange his paper money for "the real thing"). Of course, since not everyone holding dollars is likely to show up on the same day and ask to swap paper currency for gold, governments always have a little room to cheat by printing more money than the amount of gold on hand justifies. Even so, the fact that there is a finite, measurable, limited amount of gold in storage means there are limits even to this form of "inflating" the currency. Eventually, there can be no further increase in printed money without a meaningful increase in the amount of gold in storage. For the first 140 years of our history, the U.S. was on a gold standard. In 1933, Roosevelt got Congress to pass legislation that made it *illegal* for American citizens to even own gold, let alone try to swap paper dollars for it. The greatly reduced demand for gold that resulted cleared the way for the government to irresponsibly print even more paper currency (now called "federal reserve notes" rather than gold certificates). The U.S. government continued to allow foreign governments to exchange any dollars they might have for gold, but even this practice was discontinued in 1971. The last restraint on the government's unrestricted use of its money printing presses was gone.

Initial Public Offering (IPO)

is when a corporation offers to sell its stock to investors for the first time. The proceeds, less what the company owes for the broker's services, go to the company.

Institutional Investors

are organizations that trade large dollar volumes of securities on a daily basis. They include banks, pension trusts, insurance companies, and mutual funds.

Limited Liability

is one of the attractions of stock ownership. It means that shareholders have no financial obligation to assist the company should it be unable to pay its liabilities.

Over The Counter (OTC)

refers to buying and selling securities without going through a stock exchange. OTC securities are traded via a computer network that links together the brokers who are members of the National Association of Security Dealers.

Portfolio

is a collection of securities held for investment.

Preferred Stock

is a special class of stock that pays dividends at a promised rate. Holders of preferred stock must receive their dividends before any may be paid to common shareholders. They also take preference over common shareholders in receiving back the par value of the stock in the event the company is liquidated. Preferred stock typically does not carry voting rights.

Par Value

is the face value printed on a security. In the event of a corporate liquidation, preferred shareholders receive preference over common shareholders to the extent of receiving back the par value of their preferred shares.

Secondary Offering

is when a corporation offers to sell previously issued stock which is held by founders and other insiders. The proceeds, less what is owed for the broker's services, go to the individuals who are selling, not to the company.

Security

is a financial instrument that is bought and sold by the investing public. The majority are stocks, bonds, mutual funds, options, and ownership participations in limited partnerships. All publicly traded securities are subject to the regulation of the Securities & Exchange Commission.

Yield

is the effective interest rate earned on an investment expressed in annualized terms. For stocks, it is the amount of dividends per share received during the past twelve months divided by the price of the stock ($3.60/$72=5%).

Moody Press, a ministry of the Moody Bible Institute, is designed for education, evangelization, and edification. If we may assist you in knowing more about Christ and the Christian life, please write us without obligation: Moody Press, c/o MLM, Chicago, Illinois 60610.

Sound Mind Investing

THE FINANCIAL JOURNAL FOR TODAY'S CHRISTIAN FAMILY

Dear Valued Reader:

I hope this booklet has been helpful to you. If so, I believe you'd enjoy reading through a complimentary issue of my monthly *Sound Mind Investing* financial newsletter. It's based on biblically-based values and priorities (see pages 4-5), and gives you:

Help in setting and achieving realistic, personalized goals. You'll find no claims that I can predict coming economic events or market turns. Mine is a get-rich-slow, conservative strategy that emphasizes controlling your risk according to your age, goals, and personal investing temperament.

Very specific, timely advice. I recommend specific no-load mutual funds. For each of four different risk categories, I not only tell you what *what to buy* and *how much to buy*, but just as importantly, *when to sell and buy something else*!

Monthly "economic earthquake" updates. I include an economic primer that will help you understand the implications of the unfolding economic tremors. Plus, there are data and graphs of various economic indicators that will be especially helpful in giving us fair warning if a crisis seems to be approaching.

I'd like you to have the opportunity to see these benefits for yourself. Send in the attached postage-paid card for your free issue—there's absolutely no obligation to subscribe. I hope to hear from you soon!